2/11

Reptiles

Weird, wild, and wonderful

By Gary Underwood

Gareth Stevens
Publishing

Please visit our Web site **www.garethstevens.com.** For a free color catalog of all our high-quality books, call toll free 1-800-542-2595 or fax 1-877-542-2596.

Library of Congress Cataloging-in-Publication Data

Underwood, Gary.
 Reptiles / Gary Underwood.
   p. cm. — (Weird, wild, and wonderful)
 Includes index.
 ISBN 978-1-4339-3572-5 (library binding)
 1. Reptiles—Juvenile literature. I. Title.
 QL644.2.U63 2010
 597.9—dc22
                                    2009043881

Published in 2010 by
Gareth Stevens Publishing
111 East 14th Street, Suite 349
New York, NY 10003

© 2010 Blake Publishing

For Gareth Stevens Publishing:
Art Direction: Haley Harasymiw
Editorial Direction: Kerri O'Donnell

Designed in Australia by www.design-ed.com.au

Photography by Kathie Atkinson

Printed in the United States of America

CPSIA compliance information: Batch #CW10GS: For further information contact Gareth Stevens, New York, New York, at 1-800-542-2595.

Contents

What Are Reptiles?

Reptiles have lived in the wild for about 300 million years. Crocodiles, snakes, lizards, and turtles are all reptiles. It is easy to tell if an animal is a reptile. Reptiles are always covered in **scales**. They don't have feathers, fur, or hair.

Fact Bite

There are around 5,000 different types of lizards in the world. Lizards have scaly skin, four legs, ears, and a long tail. They usually see very well.

The blue-tongue lizard is one of the world's largest skinks.

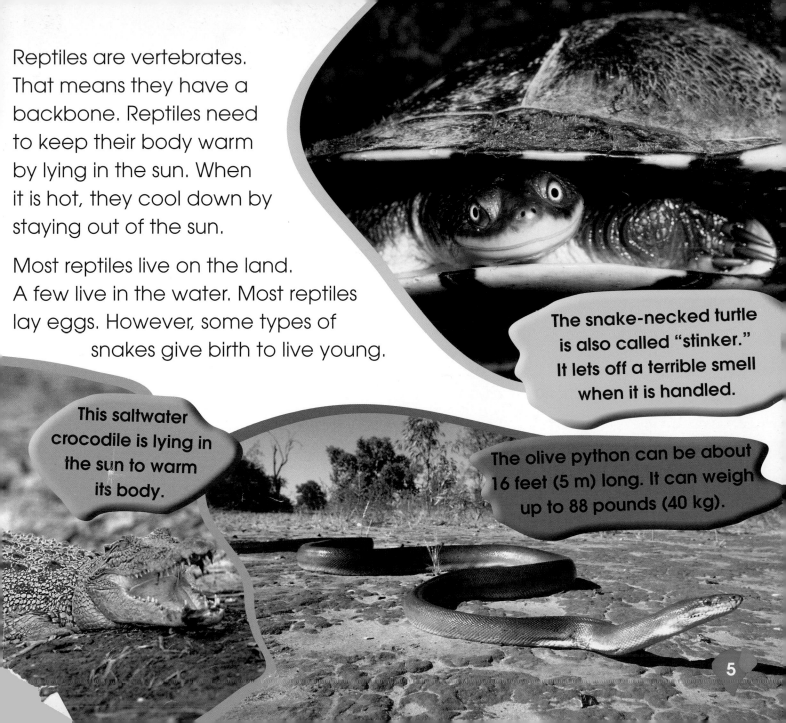

Reptiles are vertebrates. That means they have a backbone. Reptiles need to keep their body warm by lying in the sun. When it is hot, they cool down by staying out of the sun.

Most reptiles live on the land. A few live in the water. Most reptiles lay eggs. However, some types of snakes give birth to live young.

The snake-necked turtle is also called "stinker." It lets off a terrible smell when it is handled.

This saltwater crocodile is lying in the sun to warm its body.

The olive python can be about 16 feet (5 m) long. It can weigh up to 88 pounds (40 kg).

Wonderful Scales

Reptiles are covered with wonderful scales. Scales come in different shapes, sizes, and colors.

Some scales are like weird tubes. Others are flat. Sometimes scales sit beside each other. Sometimes they overlap. A reptile may have scales of different shapes or colors on different parts of its body. Wild!

Snakes and most lizards do not have eyelids. The eye is covered by a clear scale.

The thorny devil has large, pointed scales. The scales look dangerous. This helps scare away **predators**.

Scales are very important. They protect the body. Scales help some reptiles, like snakes, move. Scales keep reptiles from losing **moisture**. They also help them hide.

Fact Bites

Some reptiles change their color to hide.

Many reptiles shed their skin and grow new skin.

Skink scales

This red-bellied black snake has scales of different colors.

Why Do Reptiles Sunbathe?

Reptiles are often called "**cold-blooded**." This is not really correct. Their blood is not "cold." Reptiles get hotter or colder depending on the temperature around them. When the sun is shining, their bodies soak up the heat. They become warmer. Their bodies are cooler at night because it is cooler then.

This perentie is sunning itself on a termite mound. The perentie is Australia's biggest goanna.

Saltwater crocodile

This thorny devil soaks up warmth from the desert sand.

A reptile keeps warm by lying in the sun. That is why you will see them sunbathing on tracks, rocks, and riverbanks.

When it is hot, reptiles stay out of the sun to cool down. Crocodiles sit on riverbanks with their tails in water. They also open their **jaws** to help them cool down. Snakes and lizards hide under rocks or in holes in the ground.

The northern red-faced turtle often sunbathes on rocks and logs.

Fact Bite

Mammals, such as people, are warm-blooded. They make their own body heat. Their body temperature stays about the same all the time, whether it's hot or cold outside.

The Oldest Reptile?

Crocodiles have been around for millions of years—since the time of dinosaurs. Crocodiles still look and act like their prehistoric ancestors.

Crocodiles have a long **snout**. Their jaws have very strong muscles. These muscles help them snap their mouths shut quickly. Their jaws can crush the skull of a pig with one snap. Wild!

Freshwater crocodiles have longer, narrower snouts than saltwater crocodiles.

Fact Bites

The saltwater crocodile is the world's largest reptile.

On land, crocodiles can move as fast as 7 miles (11 km) per hour for a short time.

The crocodile is **amphibious**. It walks on land using its **webbed** feet. Its powerful tail and narrow body help it move quickly through the water.

Saltwater crocodiles have wider snouts than freshwater crocodiles.

Crocodiles have a large supply of teeth. When an old tooth falls out, a new tooth grows in its place.

11

Hide and Seek

The gaboon viper is lying in wait for its prey.

Reptiles are good at hiding. One way they hide is to blend in with their surroundings. This is called **camouflage**. This makes it harder for predators to find and eat them.

The southern leaf-tailed gecko has grainy coloring. This helps it hide on the rocks where it lives.

Some reptiles use colors to help them blend in. Some lizards can lighten and darken their color pattern. Other reptiles use the texture of their scales to help them blend in.

Camouflage is also useful when a reptile hunts for food. A disguised reptile can creep up on its prey unnoticed. Then it can pounce!

This gecko blends in with the rocks where it searches for food.

When faced with a threat, reptiles react in different ways. Some can run very fast. Others can climb trees. Some can disappear underwater.

Many lizards give off weird smells to defend themselves. Others squirt sticky liquid from their tail. Some lizards can even make their tails drop off.

The lace **monitor** can run fast. It is also an excellent tree climber. When it is scared, it will race to the nearest tree and climb it.

The bearded dragon opens its mouth very wide to help it look bigger. This scares off its enemies.

14

When threatened, a crocodile will show its teeth and yellow tongue. It will make a hissing sound. A crocodile will blow up its body to look bigger. Smaller crocodiles often stand on their tail. If that doesn't scare off the predator, they will flick their tails. Some snap their jaws together.

The frilled lizard lifts its frill around its head to frighten its enemies. It also opens its mouth wide to look scarier!

15

A reptile has an unusual tongue. It is not used to taste food or for swallowing. It is only used to smell things.

The tongue collects scents from the air. The tongue takes these scents into the mouth. It touches a smelling **organ** in the top of the mouth. This is why lizards flick their tongues in and out.

The shingleback lizard is a skink with a big, blue tongue. It feeds on fungi, dead animals, insects, berries, fruits, and flowers.

A perentie smells the air with its forked tongue.

16

Some large lizards and snakes have forked tongues. They have two small holes in the top of their mouth. That's where their smelling organs are found. Each fork of the tongue touches an organ. It is like having two smell collectors. That's why these reptiles have such a wonderful sense of smell.

This Stimson's python is using its tongue to smell for food.

A gecko's eyes are like a snake's eyes. The eyelids don't move, so the gecko licks them clean.

Blue and Scary

The blue-tongue lizard is a large skink. It has a long body, a large head, and short legs.

This lizard has a weird, blue tongue. The tongue sits in its pink mouth. When the lizard is frightened, it faces the threat. It opens its mouth wide and sticks out its fat, blue tongue. If its enemy doesn't go away, it will hiss. It will also puff up its body to look bigger.

Fact Bite

Blue-tongues can live for 30 years. They do not mind living in your garden because they eat snails, slugs, flowers, and fruit.

A blue-tongue lizard is really a big skink—with a blue tongue!

Blue-tongues have wonderful ways of smelling things. Like most lizards, they can smell using their tongue.

Blue-tongues are not poisonous, but it's best to leave them alone. A blue-tongue might bite if you pick it up.

Blue-tongues like to eat snails.

Are All Snakes Poisonous?

Snakes are long, bendy reptiles. They have no feet, arms, eyelids, or external ears. They can be from 4 inches (10 cm) to 30 feet (9 m) long.

Snakes can have a wonderful range of colors. Brightly colored snakes are usually **venomous**. The color is a warning to predators.

All snakes are carnivores. That means they eat meat. Snakes eat termites, rats, birds, frogs, and other reptiles. Snakes eat their prey whole. Their lower jaw separates from the upper jaw. This allows them to eat prey three times larger than their head.

The brown tree snake is poisonous. It comes out at night. It hides under rocks and in caves and tree hollows.

Fact Bite

Some snakes, like the boa constrictor, kill their prey by squeezing it to death.

A snake hunting at the edge of a swamp

There are 2,700 species of snakes. Of these, 375 species have venom. They inject poison through their fangs into their prey. This kills the prey or stops it from moving. Some venom is so strong it can even kill humans.

This highlands copperhead snake is very poisonous. Its bite can kill a person.

The diamond python is the farmer's friend. It visits barns and sheds to hunt mice and rats.

Fact File: Crocodiles and Alligators

Crocodiles and alligators look quite similar, but they do have differences. What are the things that are different and the same?

Crocodiles and Alligators		
Freshwater crocodile	**Saltwater crocodile**	**Alligator**
light brown color	light brown color	dark green to black color
long, narrow snout; V-shaped	long, wide snout; V-shaped	wide snout; U-shaped
maximum weight: 110 pounds (50 kg)	maximum weight: 2,200 pounds (1000 kg)	maximum weight: 990 pounds (450 kg)
average length: 8 feet (2.5 m)	average length: 19 feet (5.8 m)	average length: 14 feet (4.3 m)
lays about 12 eggs at a time	lays 40–60 eggs at a time	lays 20–80 eggs at a time
found in freshwater	lives in fresh- or slightly salty water	prefers freshwater, can survive in slightly salty water
not dangerous to humans, will rarely **attack**	will attack and kill humans	rarely dangerous to humans
mother does not guard eggs	mother guards eggs	mother guards eggs

Glossary

amphibious   animals that can move on land and in water

attack   to try to hurt something

camouflage   to blend into the surroundings

cold-blooded   an animal whose body temperature is the same as that of its surroundings

goanna   a type of large lizard

jaws   the two bones in the head of an animal that hold the teeth

moisture   small drops of water on something or in the air

monitor   a type of large lizard

organ   part of the body that has a special purpose

predators   animals that hunt other animals for food

scales   thin, flat, horny, hard plates that cover certain animals

snout   part of an animal that sticks out in front and has the nose and jaws

venomous   poisonous

webbed   joined together with skin

For Further Information

Books

Arnosky, Jim. *Slither and Crawl: Eye to Eye with Reptiles*. New York: Sterling, 2009.

Winner, Cherie. *Everything Reptile: What Kids Really Want to Know About Reptiles*. Minnetonka, MN: Books for Young Readers, 2004.

Web Sites

Reptiles
http://animals.nationalgeographic.com/animals/reptiles.html

What Is a Reptile?
http://kids.yahoo.com/animals/reptiles

Publisher's note to educators and parents: Our editors have carefully reviewed these Web sites to ensure that they are suitable for students. Many Web sites change frequently, however, and we cannot guarantee that a site's future contents will continue to meet our high standards of quality and educational value. Be advised that students should be closely supervised whenever they access the Internet.

Index